PORTLAND DIVE BARS PASSPORT

Volume 1

KC Shomler

Steven Shomler

Arthur Breur

Bonfire Books Press

Bonfire
BOOKS
Press

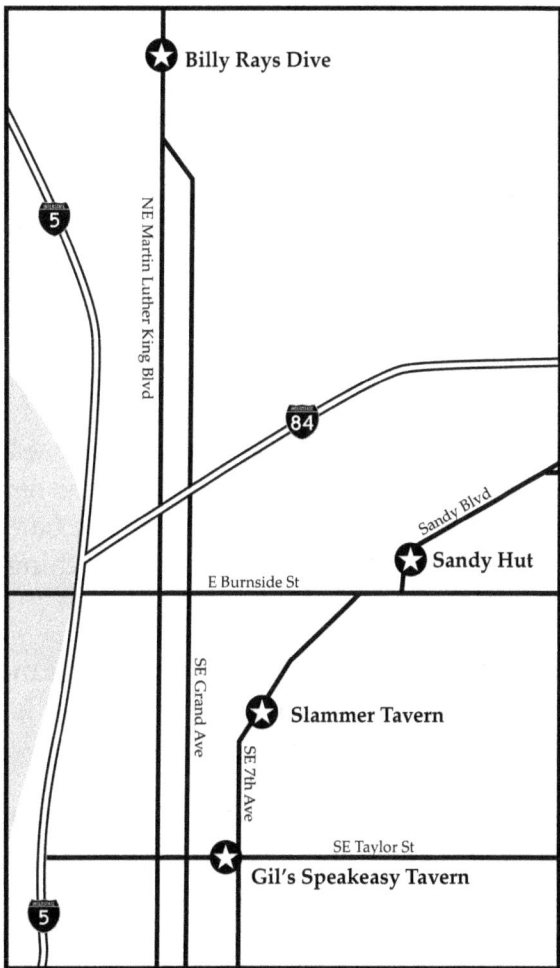

Introduction

We love dive bars! This Portland Dive Bars Passport project is our passion and privilege to bring to the masses.

We've tried to cluster bars geographically in groups of four that would be doable in one day.

We've also included at least one dive in each group that has solid food options. This here is one of the secrets to successful dive bar-in': keep your strength up with something in your stomach.

Some dive bars are good for eating, but most are not. A dive bar that serves breakfast is a rare gem, do not miss these.

Of course, you can visit these dives however you damn well please; these are merely suggestions from the pros.

Contents

Route 1

Sandy Hut
Slammer Tavern
Billy Ray's Dive
Gil's Speakeasy Tavern

Sandy Hut

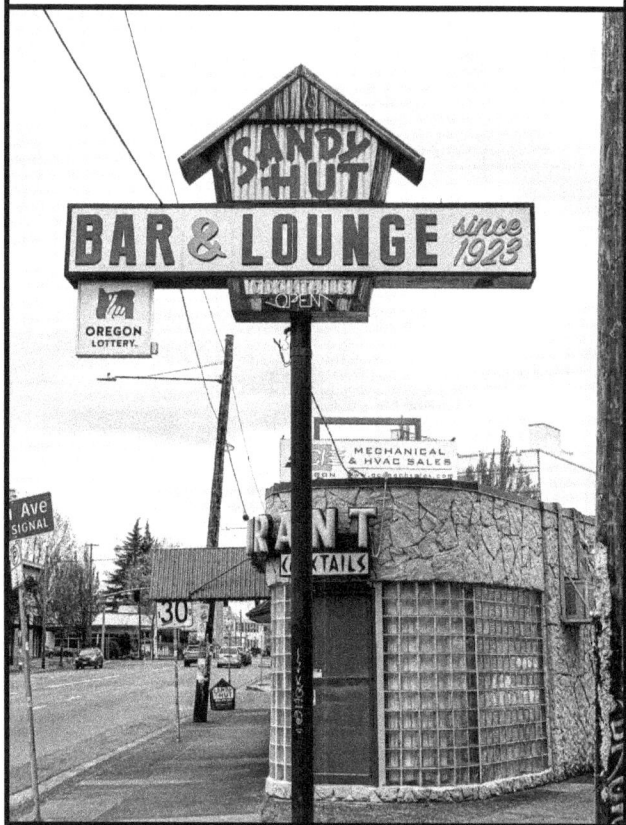

ADDRESS: 1430 NE Sandy Blvd

OUR THOUGHTS

WHY WE THINK YOU SHOULD VISIT:
Go for the retro, space age décor and check out the historic mural by Al Hirschfield.

GOOD FOR EATING OR JUST DRINKING?
Both.

YOUR TURN

DATES VISITED: _____

WORTHY OF A RETURN VISIT? _____

IMPRESSIONS: _____

_____

_____

_____

_____

_____

_____

Slammer Tavern

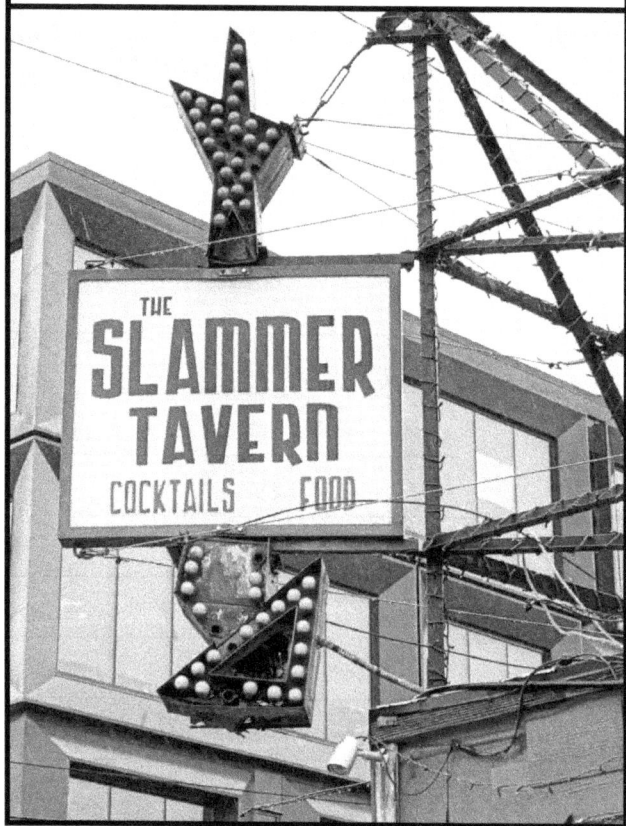

Our Thoughts

Why we think you should visit:
A dive bar where it is Christmas ALL YEAR!

Good for eating or just drinking?
Just drinking.

Your Turn

Dates Visited: _____

Worthy of a return visit? _____

Impressions: _____

_____

_____

_____

_____

_____

Billy Ray's Dive

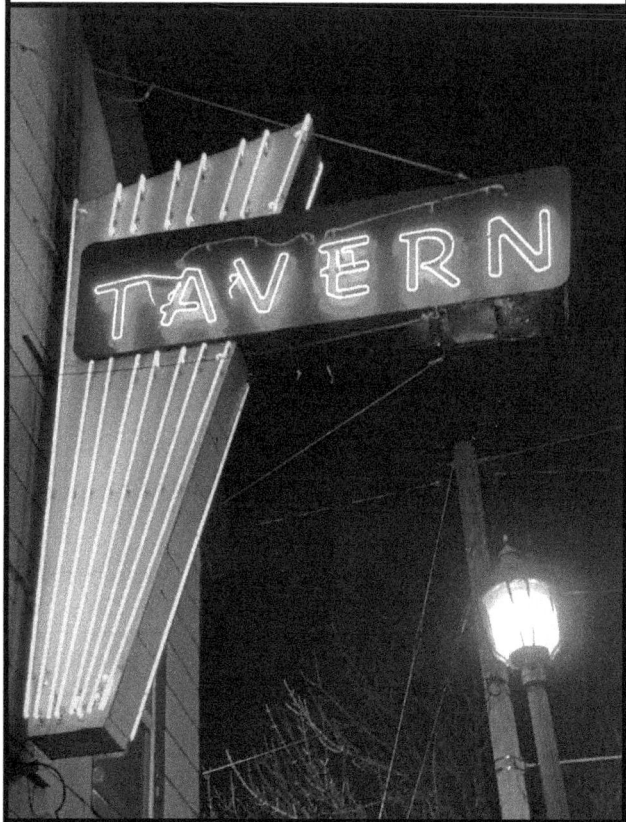

Address: 2216 NE Martin Luther King Blvd

OUR THOUGHTS

WHY WE THINK YOU SHOULD VISIT:
Solid neighborhood dive with a calm and welcoming vibe, cool copper bar.

GOOD FOR EATING OR JUST DRINKING?
Just drinking.

YOUR TURN

DATES VISITED: _____

WORTHY OF A RETURN VISIT? _____

IMPRESSIONS: _____

_____

_____

_____

_____

_____

_____

Gil's Speakeasy Tavern

ADDRESS: 609 SE Taylor St

OUR THOUGHTS

WHY WE THINK YOU SHOULD VISIT:
*Fantastic below street level dive with
amazing food and service.*

GOOD FOR EATING OR JUST DRINKING?
Just drinking.

YOUR TURN

DATES VISITED: _____

WORTHY OF A RETURN VISIT? _____

IMPRESSIONS: _____

_____

_____

_____

_____

_____

_____

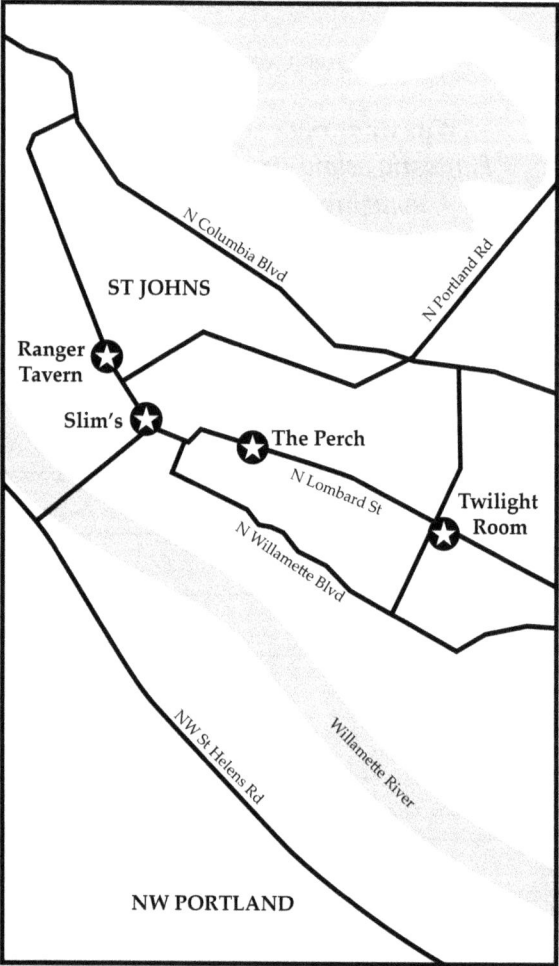

N Columbia Blvd

N Portland Rd

ST JOHNS

Ranger
Tavern

Slim's

The Perch

N Lombard St

Twilight
Room

N Willamette Blvd

NW St Helens Rd

Willamette River

NW PORTLAND

Route 2

Slim's Restaurant & Lounge
The Perch Bar & Grill
The Ranger Tavern
The Twilight Room

Slim's Restaurant & Lounge

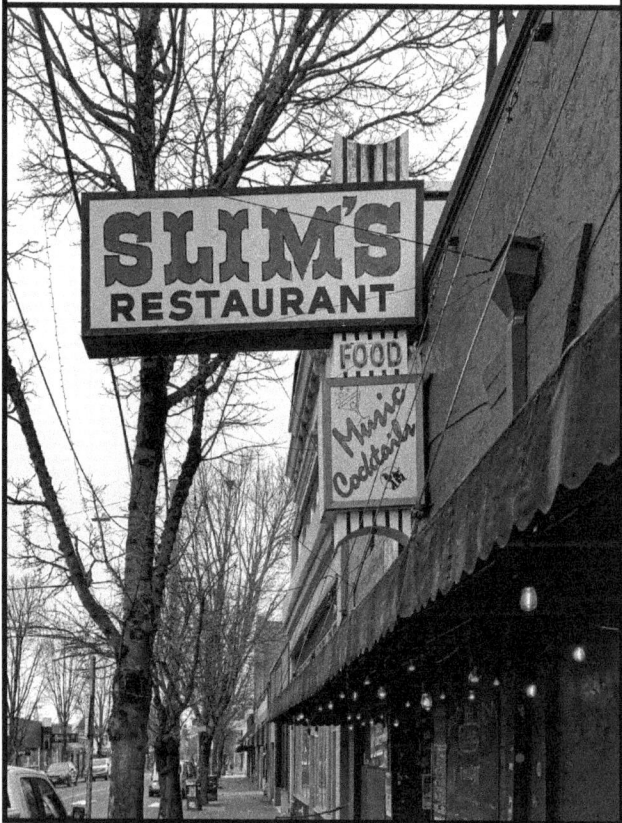

SLIM'S
RESTAURANT

FOOD

Music
Cocktails

ADDRESS: 8635 N Lombard St

OUR THOUGHTS

WHY WE THINK YOU SHOULD VISIT:
Historic dive bar with great food.

GOOD FOR EATING OR JUST DRINKING?
Both. They have breakfast!

YOUR TURN

DATES VISITED: _____

WORTHY OF A RETURN VISIT? _____

IMPRESSIONS: _____

_____

_____

_____

_____

_____

_____

The Perch Bar & Grill

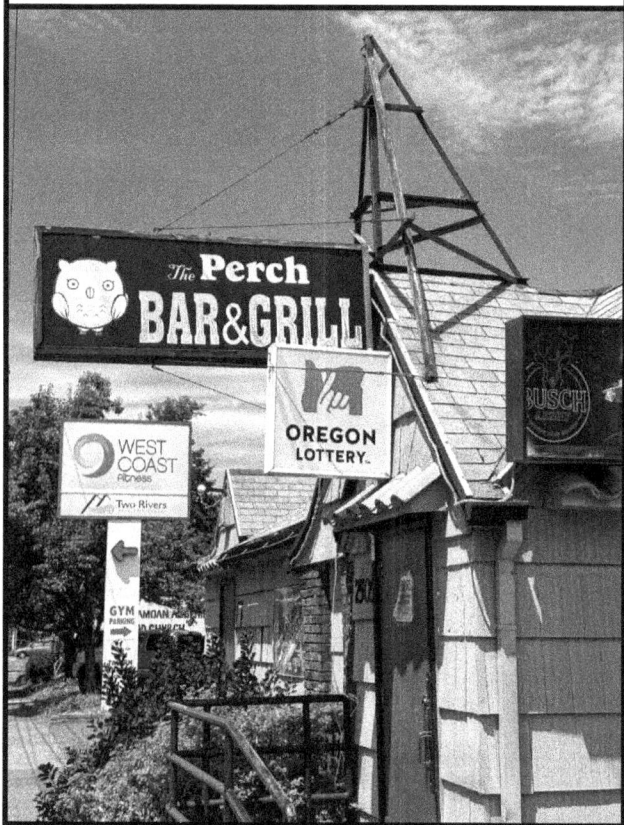

OUR THOUGHTS

WHY WE THINK YOU SHOULD VISIT:
*Cozy neighborhood joint, try to "spot"
all the owls.*

GOOD FOR EATING OR JUST DRINKING?
Just drinking.

YOUR TURN

DATES VISITED: _____

WORTHY OF A RETURN VISIT? _____

IMPRESSIONS: _____

_____

_____

_____

_____

_____

_____

The Ranger Tavern

ADDRESS: 9520 N Lombard St

OUR THOUGHTS

WHY WE THINK YOU SHOULD VISIT:
Possibly the friendliest dive bar in Portland, lots of tvs to watch 'the game.'

GOOD FOR EATING OR JUST DRINKING?
Just drinking.

YOUR TURN

DATES VISITED: _____

WORTHY OF A RETURN VISIT? _____

IMPRESSIONS: _____

_____

_____

_____

_____

_____

_____

The Twilight Room

MONDAY
DOGS EAT FREE

TUE TRIVIA 8PM FREE

Patio
NOW OPEN

Family
Dining
Entrance

ADDRESS: 5242 N Lombard St

OUR THOUGHTS

WHY WE THINK YOU SHOULD VISIT:
*Gorgeous dog-friendly patio and solid
food and drink specials.*

GOOD FOR EATING OR JUST DRINKING?
Both.

YOUR TURN

DATES VISITED: _____

WORTHY OF A RETURN VISIT? _____

IMPRESSIONS: _____

_____

_____

_____

_____

_____

_____

Route 3

Donnie Vegas
The Alibi Tiki Lounge
George's Corner Tavern
Mad Hanna

Donnie Vegas

Address: 1203 NE Alberta

OUR THOUGHTS

WHY WE THINK YOU SHOULD VISIT:
Come for the frose, stay for the artful bathroom graffiti.

GOOD FOR EATING OR JUST DRINKING?
Both, provided you like hot dogs.

YOUR TURN

DATES VISITED: _____

WORTHY OF A RETURN VISIT? _____

IMPRESSIONS: _____

_____

_____

_____

_____

_____

_____

The Alibi Tiki Lounge

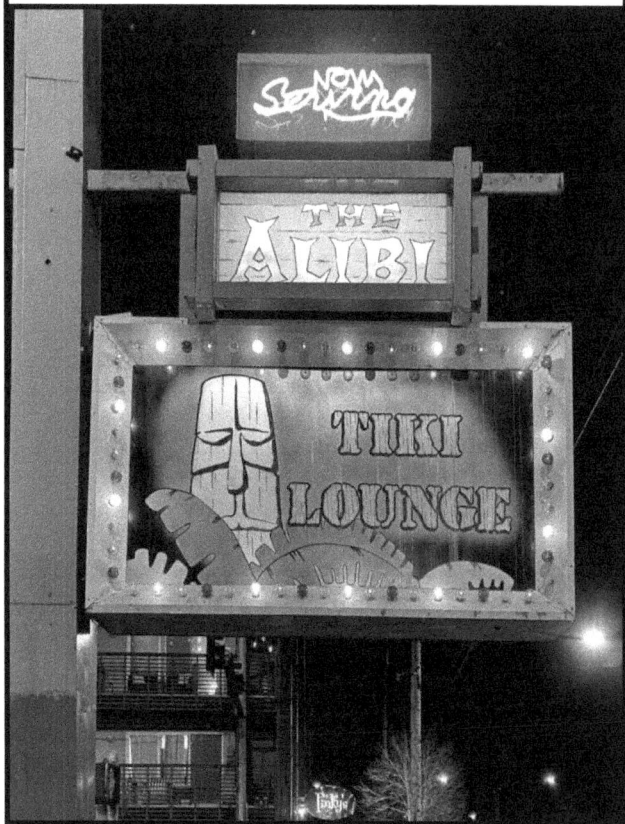

OUR THOUGHTS

WHY WE THINK YOU SHOULD VISIT:
*Fantastic tiki dive bar, not to be missed.
Seriously, go there.*

GOOD FOR EATING OR JUST DRINKING?
Both.

YOUR TURN

DATES VISITED: _____

WORTHY OF A RETURN VISIT? _____

IMPRESSIONS: _____

_____

_____

_____

_____

_____

_____

George's Corner Tavern

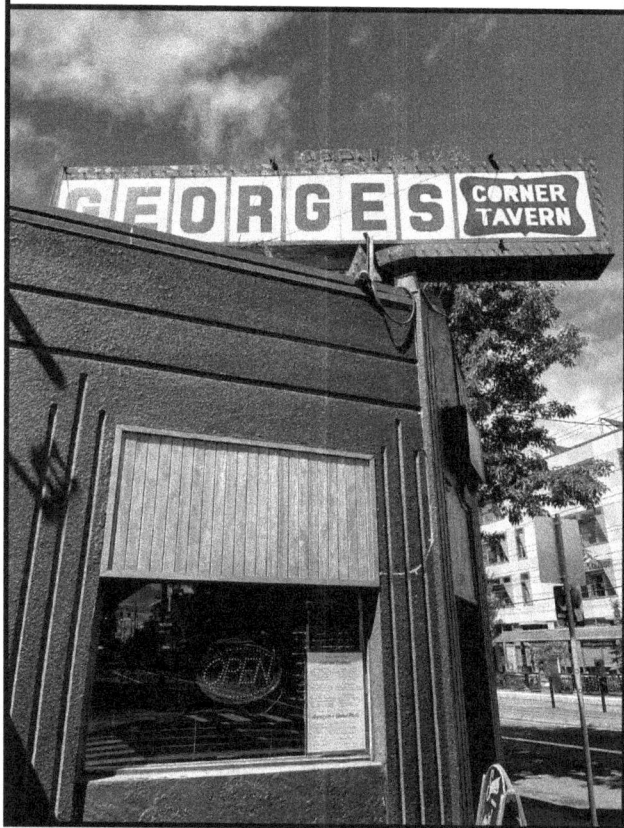

Address: 5501 N Interstate Ave

OUR THOUGHTS

WHY WE THINK YOU SHOULD VISIT:
Two words: Fried Chicken.

GOOD FOR EATING OR JUST DRINKING?
Both.

YOUR TURN

DATES VISITED: _____

WORTHY OF A RETURN VISIT? _____

IMPRESSIONS: _____

_____

_____

_____

_____

_____

_____

Mad Hanna

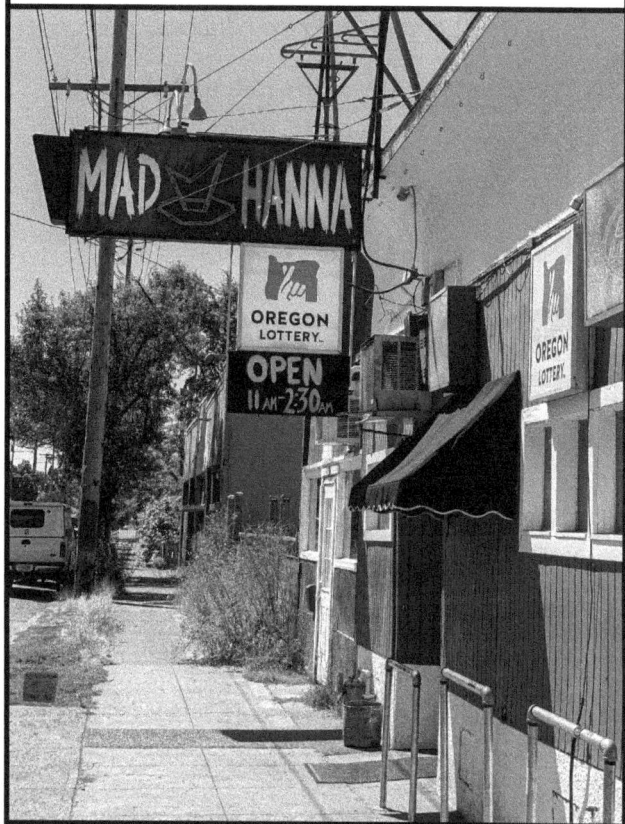

ADDRESS: 6129 NE Fremont

OUR THOUGHTS

WHY WE THINK YOU SHOULD VISIT:
*Quirky décor, general store
next door, great music.*

GOOD FOR EATING OR JUST DRINKING?
Just drinking.

YOUR TURN

DATES VISITED: _____

WORTHY OF A RETURN VISIT? _____

IMPRESSIONS: _____

_____

_____

_____

_____

_____

_____

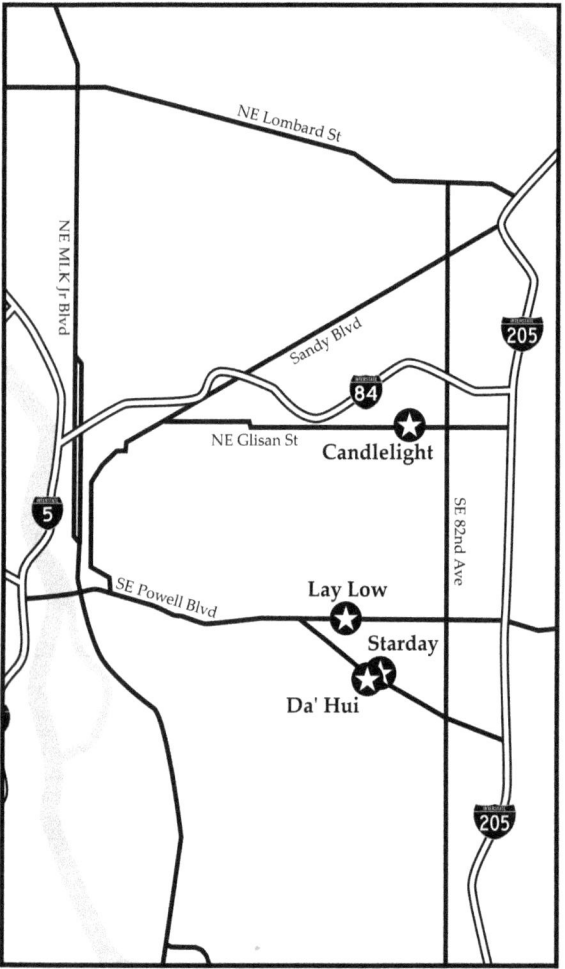

NE Lombard St

NE MLK Jr Blvd

Sandy Blvd

84

NE Glisan St
Candlelight

5

SE 82nd Ave

205

SE Powell Blvd

Lay Low

Starday

Da' Hui

205

Route 4

Da' Hui
Starday Tavern
Lay Low
Candlelight Lounge

Da' Hui

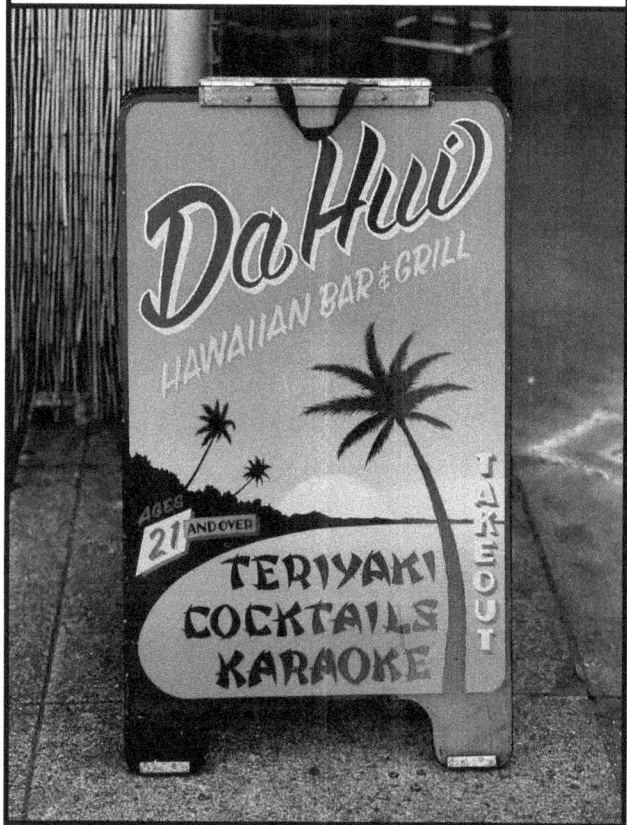

ADDRESS: 6506 SE Foster Rd

OUR THOUGHTS

WHY WE THINK YOU SHOULD VISIT:
Best Mai Tai on the mainland.
(We are suckers for tiki bars.)

GOOD FOR EATING OR JUST DRINKING?
Both.

YOUR TURN

DATES VISITED: _____

WORTHY OF A RETURN VISIT? _____

IMPRESSIONS: _____

_____

_____

_____

_____

_____

_____

Starday Tavern

ADDRESS: 6517 SE Foster Rd

OUR THOUGHTS

WHY WE THINK YOU SHOULD VISIT:
A vibrant live music calendar. It's a friendly, comfy spot, great for loafin'.

GOOD FOR EATING OR JUST DRINKING?
Just drinking.

YOUR TURN

DATES VISITED: _____

WORTHY OF A RETURN VISIT? _____

IMPRESSIONS: _____

_____

_____

_____

_____

_____

_____

Lay Low

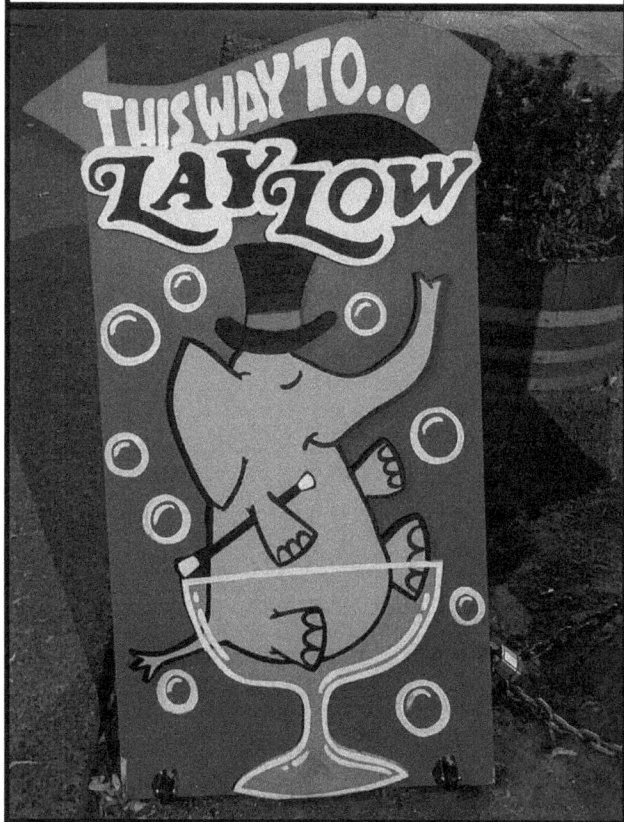

Our Thoughts

Why we think you should visit:
Tchotchke heaven, great specials.

Good for eating or just drinking?
Just drinking.

Your Turn

Dates Visited: _____

Worthy of a return visit? _____

Impressions: _____

_____

_____

_____

_____

_____

_____

Candlelight Lounge

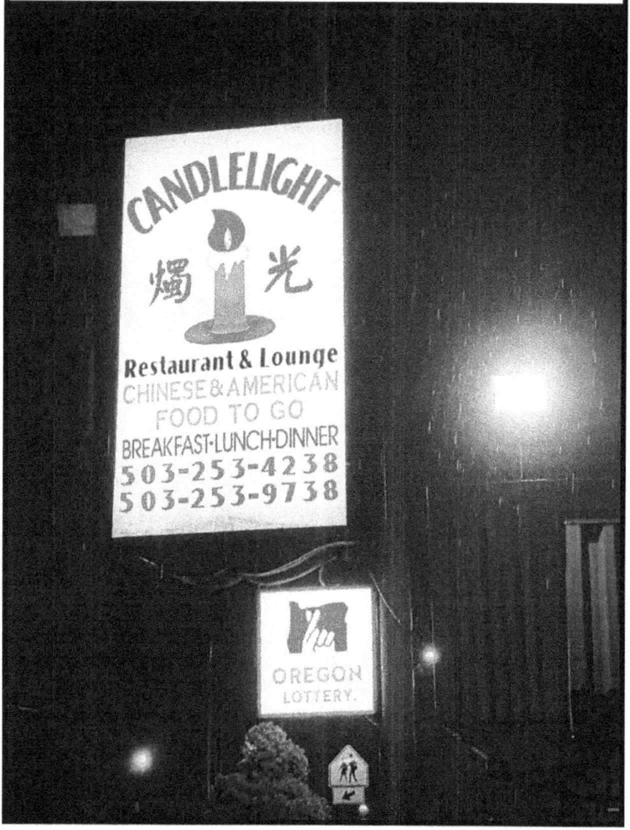

Address: 7334 NE Glisan St

Our Thoughts

Why we think you should visit:
*Dive bar hidden in the back of a
Chinese restaurant. Think late night stop.*

Good for eating or just drinking?
Both. (Breakfast everyday!)

Your Turn

Dates Visited: _____

Worthy of a return visit? _____

Impressions: _____

_____

_____

_____

_____

_____

CHECKLIST

Route 1 ☐
   Sandy Hut ☐
   Slammer Tavern ☐
   Billy Ray's Dive ☐
   Gil's Speakeasy Tavern ☐

Route 2 ☐
   Slim's Restaurant & Lounge ☐
   The Perch Bar & Grill ☐
   The Ranger Tavern ☐
   The Twilight Room ☐

Route 3 ☐
   Donnie Vegas ☐
   The Alibi Tiki Lounge ☐
   George's Corner Tavern ☐
   Mad Hanna ☐

Route 4 ☐
   Da' Hui ☐
   Starday Tavern ☐
   Lay Low ☐
   Candlelight Lounge ☐

www.ingramcontent.com/pod-product-compliance
Lightning Source LLC
Chambersburg PA
CBHW070032030426
42335CB00017B/2395